FINDING THE TITANIC

HOW IMAGES FROM THE OCEAN DEPTHS FUELLED INTEREST IN THE DOOMED SHIP

by Michael Burgan

Content Adviser: Brett Barker, PhD
Associate Professor of History
University of Wisconsin–Marathon County

a Capstone company — publishers for children

Raintree is an imprint of Capstone Global Library Limited,
a company incorporated in England and Wales having its registered office at
264 Banbury Road, Oxford, OX2 7DY – Registered company number: 6695582

www.raintree.co.uk
myorders@raintree.co.uk

Edited by Catherine Neitge
Designed by Tracy Davies McCabe and Catherine Neitge
Media Research by Svetlana Zhurkin
Library Consultation by Kathleen Baxter
Production by Laura Manthe
Originated by Capstone Global Library Limited

ISBN 978 1 4747 4850 6 (paperback)
21 20 19 18 17
10 9 8 7 6 5 4 3 2 1

British Library Cataloguing in Publication Data
A full catalogue record for this book is available from the British Library.

Acknowledgements
We would like to thank the following for permission to reproduce photographs:
Alamy: Collection Christophel, 47, 59 (left), Entertainment Pictures, 51, John
Frost Newspapers, 23; Dreamstime: Jaroslaw Kilian, 15, 56 (top); Getty Images:
Bettmann, 12, Ralph White, 43, Topical Press Agency, 19; National Geographic
Creative: Emory Kristof, cover, 8, 26, 36, 42, 55; Newscom: Abaca/PA Photos, 39,
akg-images, 21, Album/20th Century Fox, 45, Heritage Images/Ann Ronan Picture
Library, 18, picture-alliance/dpa/Chris Melzer, 53, World History Archive, 25, Zuma
Press/Alpha, 49, 58, Zuma Press/Keystone Pictures USA, 11, 13, 29, 56 (bottom),
Zuma Press/National News, 41; Shutterstock: Everett Historical, 5, 9, 59 (right);
Woods Hole Oceanographic Institution, 7, 31, 33, 34, 35, 57; XNR Productions, 17

Every effort has been made to contact copyright holders of material reproduced in
this book. Any omissions will be rectified in subsequent printings if notice is given
to the publisher.

All the internet addresses (URLs) given in this book were valid at the time of going
to press. However, due to the dynamic nature of the internet, some addresses may
have changed, or sites may have changed or ceased to exist since publication.
While the author and publisher regret any inconvenience this may cause readers,
no responsibility for any such changes can be accepted by either the author or the
publisher.

Printed and bound in China.

CONTENTS

ChapterOne
SEARCHING FOR THE *TITANIC*

Robert Ballard looked out over the North Atlantic Ocean and wondered whether he would find what he was looking for. Somewhere beneath the *Knorr*, the ship that had carried him to this spot, lay the remains of the *Titanic*. After years of research, Ballard was convinced he had found the area where the great steamship had come to rest more than 70 years earlier. On the night of 14 April 1912, as it made its first voyage, the *Titanic* had struck an iceberg almost 645 kilometres (400 miles) southeast of Newfoundland, Canada. A few hours after midnight on 15 April the ship sank nearly 4 km (2.5 miles) before settling on the ocean floor. Of the more than 2,200 passengers and crew, only 705 had survived.

Ballard knew that time was running out to find the *Titanic* on this trip. The US Navy had paid for him to find and investigate two of its submarines that had sunk during the 1960s. After Ballard finished that search, he could use whatever time was left on his three-week assignment to hunt for the *Titanic*. Now, on the night of 31 August 1985, Ballard had only a few days left to find the wreck. And a storm was approaching.

Ballard had once said that with the proper equipment and crew, finding the *Titanic* would be

easy. But now he began to wonder. The equipment for his expedition included sophisticated sonar on board the French research ship *Le Suroit*. Sonar uses sound waves to locate objects underwater. A device called a transducer sends out the waves. When a wave hits an object, it bounces back to the transducer as an "echo" that can be seen on a screen. *Le Suroit* towed an advanced side-scan sonar, which can locate objects on the ocean floor. Fan-shaped sound waves radiate out from what is called a towfish. The waves' echoes appear on a screen as areas of light and dark, depending on their strength. Light patches indicate the sonar has found something sticking out from the bottom. After several weeks of searching, however, *Le Suroit* had not found the *Titanic* in the area where Ballard thought it would be.

He had then turned to the next piece of underwater technology: a sledge-like submersible called *Argo*. Also known as a remotely operated vehicle (ROV), *Argo* let Ballard safely study the ocean floor for long periods in the dangerously strong water pressure. Ballard, an oceanographer who specialized in geology, had just built *Argo* with a team of engineers at the Woods Hole Oceanographic Institution in Massachusetts, USA. The *Titanic* project gave him a chance to test it.

Argo was equipped with video cameras that used technology developed by the US military. The cameras could detect natural light and magnify it 10,000 times. With the cameras, Ballard later wrote, he could "literally see in the dark". That capability was crucial at 3,810 metres (12,500 feet), because at that great depth only faint traces of sunlight reach the

The submersible *Argo* was named after the vessel that carried Jason in the Greek myth about Jason's quest for the golden fleece.

ocean's bottom. *Argo* was attached to the *Knorr* by a cable called a tether. Inside the cable were wires that carried information back and forth between the submersible and the ship's crew. The crew members controlled *Argo*'s movement and reviewed the images from its cameras.

Along with *Argo*, Ballard and his crew were also using a device called ANGUS, short for Acoustically Navigated Geological Underwater Survey. Towed by

the *Knorr*, ANGUS carried cameras it could use while hovering above the ocean floor. Unlike with *Argo*, however, Ballard and others on the surface ship could not see the images straight away. First they had to retrieve ANGUS from the ocean and then develop its film. But the pictures it took provided information about large areas of the ocean's floor. If *Argo* could find the *Titanic*, ANGUS's cameras would provide detailed photos of the wreckage.

Ballard and his team had first searched a rectangular area near where the *Titanic*'s radio

The research ship *Knorr* logged more than 2.2 million km (1.4 million miles) during the 44 years it carried scientists around the world. The US Navy ship was retired from service in 2014.

The few passengers who made it to the lifeboats watched as the *Titanic* sank beneath the waves. The image is based on an illustration from a 1912 London newspaper.

operator reported the ship's position after hitting the iceberg. Another key marker was the place where the passenger ship *Carpathia* found the *Titanic*'s lifeboats. Ballard had to take into account the speed of the ocean current on the night of 14 April 1912, because the current had carried the lifeboats away from the spot where the *Titanic* sank. After the first search with the sonar on *Le Suroit*, Ballard decided to shift the search field to the east.

Argo began to search in the new area on 28 August. Working in shifts, the crew guided *Argo* and studied its video images around the clock.

Steering *Argo* required great skill, so the crew had to strike the right balance of speed and height off the ocean floor. They wanted to get the best images possible without crashing the submersible into any obstacles.

The crew also battled a technical problem with the tether that connected the submersible to the *Knorr*. For a while, the glitch left the submersible stuck on the ocean floor. The tether was in danger of breaking, which would have left *Argo* there forever. Ballard and others quickly worked to repair the tether before it snapped. Ballard later recalled, "Covered in grease, our knuckles bleeding, we all knew this was a desperate race against time." But even if the crew could keep the tether from breaking, there was no guarantee that the wires inside it that guided *Argo* would still work. Luck, though, was on the team's side. As the *Knorr* slightly increased its speed, *Argo* broke free of the ocean floor. And while the outer covering of the tether had been damaged, the wires inside were fine. The hunt for the *Titanic* continued.

On 31 August the *Knorr* crew members on the day watch who were controlling *Argo* found nothing. That night, studying the seas, Ballard wondered whether he had simply picked the wrong spot. There was also a chance that an undersea earthquake decades before had stirred up mud that now covered the *Titanic*'s remains.

"Covered in grease, our knuckles bleeding, we all knew this was a desperate race against time."

SECRET MISSION REVEALED

The nuclear submarine Scorpion *was lost in May 1968 with 99 sailors onboard.*

At the time Robert Ballard was searching for the *Titanic*, the US Navy wanted the world to believe that the mission was just a test for the *Argo*. In part that was true, but it took several decades for the whole truth to become known. Ballard and his crew were part of a secret mission to study the remains of two nuclear submarines, the *Thresher* and the *Scorpion*. The Navy feared that the subs could be releasing radiation, a deadly form of energy. The Navy also wanted to learn whether one of the subs had been damaged in a military attack.

During the 1960s, when the subs sank, the United States was in the middle of the Cold War. It was a struggle with the Soviet Union to gain influence with other nations around the world. The Cold War was still going on in 1985, so the Navy did not want the Soviet government or anyone else to know what Ballard was doing. "The Navy never expected me to find the *Titanic*," he said years later, "and so when that happened, they got really nervous because of the publicity."

Ballard's investigation showed that the subs' nuclear reactors were intact and not leaking radiation. The visual evidence he gathered also suggested that one of the subs, the *Scorpion*, had not come under enemy fire as some had suspected. Ballard's work for the Navy helped him learn how debris settles on the ocean floor when a ship sinks – information that influenced how he searched for the *Titanic*'s debris field.

Shortly after midnight, Ballard went to his cabin. In the control room where the crew guided *Argo*, Stu Harris watched the video monitor that showed what *Argo*'s cameras saw. Harris had been *Argo*'s chief designer. Just before 1 am he said, "There's something." The rest of the crew in the control room snapped to attention as Harris switched the view to a different camera with a zoom lens. "Wreckage!" video operator Bill Lange said. He was one of three people on the ship that was filming the expedition. Soon everyone in the room was shouting with excitement as *Argo* detected more debris, including one of *Titanic*'s huge boilers. Twenty-four of the boilers, each almost 5 metres (16 feet) in diameter and 6 m (20 feet) long, along with five smaller ones, had generated the steam that powered the mammoth ship's engines.

No one wanted to leave the control room as *Argo* discovered the pieces of the *Titanic*. Finally, the ship's cook, who had just happened to stroll into the room, was chosen to tell Ballard what was happening. He found Ballard still awake, reading a book. "The guys think you should come down to the van," he said. Ballard jumped up and ran through the ship. When he entered the control room, the crew played the videotape that *Argo* had just shot. Ballard, too, could easily see the *Titanic*'s massive boiler. He knew the rest of the wreckage was probably not far away. Once again, the crew erupted with cheers.

Robert Ballard

A camera onboard ANGUS captured a fish swimming over the bow of the *Titanic.*

Argo detected more wreckage, and Ballard realized that a 12-year quest was finally over. He also thought about the more than 1,500 people who had died when the *Titanic* sank. He later wrote, "Images from the night of the disaster – a story I now knew by heart – flashed through my mind with painful intensity."

The discovery of the *Titanic* in September 1985 began the process of answering some of the lingering questions about the ship's final hours. The pictures and video Ballard brought back helped stir new interest in the ship's voyage and its resting spot. That interest remains strong today.

ChapterTwo
THE BEST OF ITS DAY

On 10 April 1912, the *Titanic*'s first paying passengers came on board as the ship prepared to sail from Southampton to New York on its maiden voyage. After short stops in Cherbourg, France, and Queenstown (now Cobh), Ireland, the steamship began its 5,000-km (3,100-mile) journey across the Atlantic.

The more than 1,300 passengers and almost 900 crew members on the *Titanic* sailed on a ship hailed as an engineering marvel. Built for England's White Star Line, it was the longest ship afloat, at about 269 m (883 feet). If stood upright, it would have been as tall as an 11-storey building. While slower than the steamships of the rival Cunard Line, the *Titanic* was considered the height of luxury. Passengers were divided into three classes, with the first-class passengers receiving the best food and fanciest cabins. But even those in third class travelled more comfortably than on other vessels, at a time when travelling by ship was the only way to cross the Atlantic.

The wealthiest passengers on the maiden voyage included US multi-millionaire John Jacob Astor and Isidor Straus, co-owner of Macy's department store in New York. White Star Line provided fine wines

A poster advertised travel on the White Star Line's *Titanic*.

and cigars for its first-class passengers, and most of the rich travelled with servants. On the lower decks, many of the third-class passengers were immigrants seeking a new life in the United States.

Along with luxury, the *Titanic* seemed to offer safety. It had 16 watertight compartments that could be sealed by electrically controlled doors. If an accident happened and water entered one compartment, Captain Edward Smith could immediately shut the doors. The ship was also designed to stay afloat if the first four compartments filled with water. Not all the doors were part of the system, and many of them still had to be closed by hand. But to several newspapers of the day, the *Titanic* seemed safe, and *Shipbuilder* magazine called it "practically unsinkable". And although White Star Line did not make that claim before the ship sailed, a company official repeated it when news of the sinking first reached shore.

After the ship steamed away from Ireland, the passengers had several days to enjoy the food, listen to the ship's band and swim in the pool. In letters and journals, several passengers wrote about how smooth the voyage was. "There was nothing to indicate that we were on the stormy Atlantic Ocean," Colonel Archibald Gracie wrote. Most of the passengers didn't know about the reports of icebergs in the ocean that the *Titanic* received on 14 April.

The sky that night was moonless, and no wind stirred the ocean's surface. If there had been wind, it would have pushed waves into any iceberg ahead of the ship, creating foam and making the ice easier to spot. Moonlight, too, would have made it easier to see

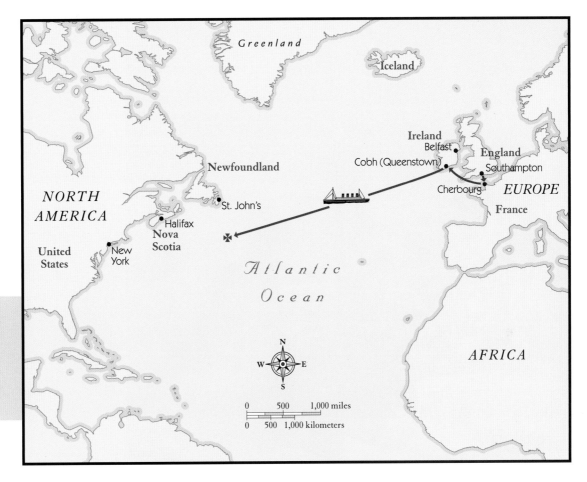

Most passengers on the doomed ship boarded the *Titanic* in Southampton.

an iceberg. Given the conditions, lookout Frederick Fleet, standing in the ship's crow's nest, was surprised to suddenly spot something ahead of the ship. Just after 11.40 pm, he rang a bell three times and then phoned the bridge with a dire message: "Iceberg right ahead".

On the ship's bridge, which was the control room of the *Titanic*, First Officer William Murdoch gave orders to steer hard to the left and reverse the engines. The *Titanic*, though, was travelling too fast to avoid the iceberg. In about 30 seconds, the grand ship's starboard (right) side brushed against an

Pieces of the iceberg hit the *Titanic*'s deck as the huge ship scraped the iceberg underwater.

iceberg that some on board estimated was about 30 m (100 feet) tall. A few tonnes of ice fell from the iceberg onto the ship. Even though the *Titanic* avoided a head-on collision, that glancing impact was enough to open a gash in the ship's metal hull. Below the ocean's surface, water began to pour in.

Captain Edward Smith

Most passengers didn't realize that the ship had struck an iceberg, though some who were out on deck saw it as the *Titanic* passed by. A few people also noticed a slight vibration with the impact, while others heard a grinding or ripping sound. Below decks, though, the crew could see the water pouring into the ship. It began to fill six of the front watertight compartments. Within 20 minutes after the *Titanic* hit the iceberg, Captain Smith feared his ship was doomed.

The captain ordered the radio operator to send out a distress signal, and some of the crew launched flares called distress rockets in an effort to alert nearby ships. The closest ship was the *Californian*. How close was never established, with estimates ranging from 8 to 32 km (5 to 20 miles). Its radio operator had gone to bed for the night and so didn't receive the distress call. But some of its crew saw the flares and tried to use a lamp to contact the mystery ship they could see in the distance but could not recognize. They had no luck. Further away was the *Carpathia*, which received the *Titanic*'s radio distress signal and turned towards the damaged vessel.

Throughout the ship, passengers put on life jackets and began making their way to the lifeboats. The path was easier for the first-class passengers, because their cabins were close to the boats, which were on the upper decks. Third-class passengers were much lower, and barriers in parts of the ship prevented them from easily moving to the higher decks. As was the custom then, third-class passengers were not allowed to enter the parts of the ship meant for wealthier passengers.

People studying the *Titanic* disaster have offered many theories on why the ship hit the iceberg, but human error certainly played a large role. The ship was probably going too fast, given that Captain Smith knew other ships had spotted ice in the area. He might have been more cautious if he had received all the reports of ice that came in over the radio, but some never reached the bridge. But even those reports wouldn't have told him that his ship was approaching an ice field that was 120 km (75 miles) long.

The large loss of life that night also could have been avoided if the ship had carried enough lifeboats for all of its passengers and crew – but it didn't. The *Titanic*'s designers seemed to think that more boats wouldn't be needed because the ship was so watertight that it almost certainly couldn't sink. Lives were also lost because some passengers refused the order to board the lifeboats. They may have feared bobbing in the tiny boats on the cold ocean in the darkness, or perhaps they still believed that the *Titanic* was unsinkable. The ship's crew kept some men from boarding the boats, following an order to

The lifeboats lowered from the *Titanic* were not always full. More lives could have been saved.

let women and children go first. Partly for that reason, many lifeboats entered the water half full or less.

As the passengers and some crew members boarded the lifeboats, the *Titanic* was clearly sinking. Realizing this, more people tried to escape, but some passengers simply accepted the fact that death was near. Others refused to be separated from their loved ones. When officers tried to put Ida Straus on a lifeboat without her husband, Isidor, she wouldn't go. "No, I will not be separated from my husband," she said. "As we have lived, so we will die, together." Others waited too long to board a lifeboat; by 2.05 am on 15 April, all the boats had gone, leaving about 1,500 people still on board. Some jumped from the sinking ship and managed to reach a lifeboat at sea, but most drowned when the ship sank. Captain Smith, following seafaring tradition, went down with his ship.

News of the *Titanic*'s sinking flashed around the world. *The New York Times* captured what many people were experiencing – a "feeling of amazement that this great, new ship could be so soon lost, and lost in that way." The *Times* writer, like many people, thought the *Titanic*'s technical advancements should have prevented "one of the greatest disasters of the sea". Part of the shock came as people realized that their faith in ever-continuing progress might have been misplaced. New and better engineering and technology could not prevent disasters – or the human error that could help cause them. That faith in human progress was battered again with the coming of World War I two years later and the millions of deaths it caused. The *Titanic* disaster also showed that tragedy can hit everyone equally, rich or poor. The millionaires John Jacob Astor and Isidor Straus were among the dead.

The front page of *The New York Times* carried the grim news of the *Titanic* disaster.

Both the British and US governments investigated the disaster. The British investigation's final report blamed the collision on "the excessive speed at which the ship was being navigated". It and the American report faulted the *Californian* for not responding to the distress rockets its crew saw. The investigations led to new laws requiring ships to carry enough lifeboats for all passengers and crew.

In the years after the *Titanic*'s sinking, interest in the disaster faded. World War I, with its nearly 18 million deaths, started in Europe in 1914, and then other events caught the world's attention. Renewed interest in the *Titanic* came in 1955, when Walter Lord's book *A Night to Remember* was published. His account of the sinking included observations from some of the survivors. A film based on Lord's book showed passengers realizing that they faced death. Although there had been earlier films about the disaster, *A Night to Remember* was the most historically accurate.

The film came out in 1958, when Robert Ballard was a teenager in California. Already fascinated by the sea, he learned how to scuba dive so he could study life below the ocean's surface. When Ballard was 19, his father helped him get a job at a company that was developing a three-man deep-sea submarine for the US government. After college, Ballard served in the US Navy, which assigned him to Woods Hole Oceanographic Institution. He remained there after his military service and continued his education. Talking with others who did extremely deep dives and underwater research, Ballard became interested in doing his own research far below the ocean's surface. He also began to think about searching for the wreck of the *Titanic*. Having been interested in the sea since childhood, he knew about the ship's

Kenneth MORE in
A NIGHT TO REMEMBER

TITANIC
LIVERPOOL

The much-praised 1958 film *A Night to Remember,* which starred British actor Kenneth More, was based on Walter Lord's very successful book.

history. As he learned more, he also became drawn to the human side of the story. He learned about the lives of those who survived and those who died.

Ballard made many dives in *Alvin*, a three-man sub built for the US Navy. He realized that scientists needed better ways to capture images 4 km (2.5 miles) underwater. Using remotely operated vehicles would be safer than diving to the ocean's depths. He thought he could get money for what eventually became *Argo* by suggesting that he would use his creation to search for the *Titanic*.

PHOTOGRAPHIC PARTNER

Emory Kristof photographed Robert Ballard (standing, in cap) studying search videos aboard the Knorr.

As Robert Ballard began to think seriously about searching for the *Titanic*, he often worked with Emory Kristof, a photographer for *National Geographic* magazine. The two met in 1974 when Ballard was part of an expedition to explore an underwater mountain range in the Atlantic using *Alvin* and other submersibles. Kristof saw that the technology scientists were using for underwater photography was old and that they didn't use the best techniques when shooting. "If we were to work with some of these science groups," he said in a 2011 interview, "and just apply what we knew from shallow water [photography], we could improve the quality of the deep ocean pictures."

Kristof also helped to design the cameras used on ANGUS and the equipment that made it possible to develop its photos while a research ship was at sea. Ballard later wrote that Kristof "came to share my dream of finding the *Titanic*". The photographer was on the *Knorr* when Ballard found the *Titanic,* and he later took a submersible down to the wreck to photograph it. He continued to help develop new technology to take better pictures underwater.

Ballard persuaded Woods Hole in 1977 to let him use a ship that had a long metal pipe to send cameras and sonar to the sea bottom. It lacked the flexibility *Argo* would later give him, but it was a start. Unfortunately, a mechanical mistake led to the pipe's breaking, destroying the cameras and other equipment. Ballard put his search for the *Titanic* on hold for a few years and spent some of the time designing and building *Argo*.

Ballard was not the only person trying to find the *Titanic*. A millionaire named Jack Grimm organized an expedition to find the ship in 1980. Working with two top oceanographers, Grimm's crew tried to locate the *Titanic* using sonar. But on three expeditions, Grimm and his team found nothing.

Ballard followed the news of Grimm's searches. He came to see that Grimm did not always know where to look and did not trust the scientists he hired. The scientists thought poorly of some of Grimm's ideas. Grimm also had the bad luck to sail in horrible weather on each try. Still, those missions led to the first mapping of parts of the ocean near where the *Titanic* sank. And Ballard was able to see some of the information gathered by Grimm's team. He realized that he would have to search some of the same area, just to be sure Grimm had not missed anything. In June 1985, *Argo* was ready, and Ballard hoped he would succeed where Grimm had failed.

ChapterThree
DEEPER INTO THE WRECKAGE

When his years of hard work and preparation finally paid off on 1 September 1985, Robert Ballard celebrated with his crew. But the mood on the *Knorr* quickly changed. Time had passed since the crew realized it had found the *Titanic*, and now it was close to 2 am – just 20 minutes before the time of day when the ocean liner sank. Ballard told the crew he was going out on deck. They followed him, and at 2.20 am he led the crew in a moment of silence for the people who had died in the cold Atlantic waters on 15 April 1912. After five or ten minutes he said, "Thank you all. Now let's get back to work."

Through the day on 1 September *Argo* continued to explore the debris field. Ballard and his team also found the main part of the *Titanic* wreck. After locating the ship, Ballard grabbed the charts that showed where it rested. He wanted as few people as possible to know the exact location, so others would not damage the site or try to retrieve artifacts.

Argo began to explore the main wreck on 2 September and that brought new worries. Not knowing what *Argo* would find, Ballard realized that the mini-sub could crash into the ship before the crew could steer it out of trouble. But *Argo* moved smoothly over the wreckage, sending back images

A camera onboard ANGUS photographed anchor chains on the bow of the doomed *Titanic.*

of the bridge, where Captain Edward Smith had once stood. *Argo*'s videotaping lasted only about six minutes, but it showed that a large part of the ship was still intact. On another pass, *Argo*'s images revealed that the stern (rear) of the ship had broken off from the main part. The two sections were almost 610 m (2,000 feet) apart on the ocean floor.

The storm that Ballard had seen coming finally hit, and he ordered *Argo* out of the water. ANGUS, though, could handle rougher seas, so the next day it went down to further explore what *Argo* had found. It came back to the surface with thousands of colour photos showing items from the ship that had survived the sinking, such as a teacup, wine bottles and a silver tray. Then the *Knorr* passed over the main wreck, so ANGUS could capture details of it. When the film was developed, the images were blurry. The camera-toting sledge had been too high above the wreck to get good pictures. As the time to leave the region approached, Ballard sent ANGUS down one last time. The crew battled stiff winds and high seas as they launched the sledge, which sank to just 4 m (13 feet) or so above the *Titanic*. This time it returned with clear colour pictures of the wreck. With the mission a success, the *Knorr* prepared to return to Woods Hole, Massachusetts.

On 6 September a helicopter appeared above the *Knorr* as it sailed towards its home port. Three US television networks had hired the helicopter so it could retrieve images of the *Titanic*. Soon some of the pictures and videos taken 4 km (2.5 miles) below the surface of the Atlantic Ocean appeared in newspapers and on TV sets around the world, creating a strong interest in the ship.

Soon it became possible to get even better images of the *Titanic*, thanks to improved technology and another ROV that Ballard and his engineers developed. The submersible, called *Jason Jr*, would let Ballard explore inside the wreckage. Sailing in the summer of 1986 on the *Atlantis II*, Ballard brought

Jason Jr photographed **Alvin** pulling alongside the **Titanic**.

along the submersible *Alvin*. From *Alvin*, Ballard and crew would launch *Jason Jr*, which was nicknamed *JJ*.

Alvin had been rebuilt since its launch in 1964. The Navy replaced its steel shell with titanium, a much stronger metal, in 1973. That allowed *Alvin* to go even deeper, where the water pressure is much stronger than it is near the surface. At the deepest ocean depths, the pressure is as forceful as a 7.3 metric tonne (8-ton) weight on an area 6.5 square centimetres (1 square inch) in size. If an accident let that much pressure into *Alvin*, its crew would instantly be killed. More changes to the submersible were made just before the 1986 expedition. The mini-sub was now controlled by a joystick connected to new electronics.

Once again the US Navy backed the expedition, and Ballard used *Jason Jr* to further explore the wrecks of the submarines *Thresher* and *Scorpion*. Then *Atlantis II* headed for the spot where Ballard had found the *Titanic*. On the first dive, technical problems forced *Alvin* to return to the surface before its three-man crew could launch *Jason Jr.* The ROV was connected to *Alvin* by a tether about 55 m (180 feet) long. As with *Argo*, the cable carried wires that let the crew control *JJ*'s movements. The crew also controlled *Jason Jr*'s camera and watched the video it recorded. In the era before digital media, the video images were stored on tape. *Alvin* also had video and still cameras and lights to cut through the ocean bottom's darkness.

On the second dive, Ballard and his crew touched bottom near the *Titanic* and got a better look at it. It took *Alvin* more than two hours to make the dive, with the temperature inside the submersible falling as they went down. The crew had put on extra clothing to stay warm.

On the ocean floor, Ballard could see that the *Titanic* was partly buried in the mud. The men spotted windows that still contained glass, and

The discovery of rusticles on the *Titanic* prompted research scientists to study the microscopic bacteria eating the iron.

they saw rust throughout the ship. Some it of had formed into long points, like icicles, that Ballard called rusticles. The rusticles were left behind after bacteria in the water had eaten the iron in the ship. Other creatures, including tiny shellfish, had eaten much of the ship's wood. The crew explored with *Alvin*, moving from spot to spot among the wreckage, but another technical problem prevented them from launching *Jason Jr.*

Jason Jr, referred to by Ballard as a "swimming eyeball", investigated a porthole on the *Titanic*.

On the third dive everything went according to plan. *JJ* explored the Grand Staircase, one of the fanciest areas in the first-class part of the ship. Inside *Alvin*, Ballard and his crew saw that a delicate light fixture had survived the plunge to the ocean's bottom. On other dives, *JJ* peered into portholes and explored the crow's nest. Will Sellers, the pilot for two of the dives, said the ROV "entered what we thought was the first officer's quarters. The whole scene here was in an eerie black-and-white, as most of the paint was long gone. Visibility was low due to all the floating rust particles that *JJ*'s tether had knocked loose."

AN EARLIER DISCOVERY

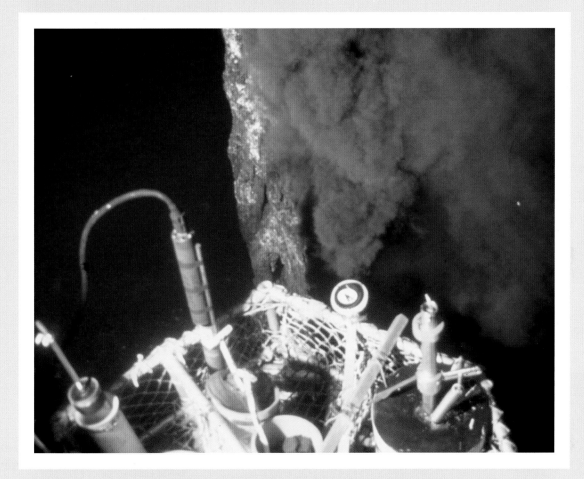

Scientists using Alvin *discovered black smokers in the depths of the Pacific Ocean.*

Finding the *Titanic* made Robert Ballard famous. But in the world of oceanography, an earlier mission of his was more important for science. In the late 1970s, he was part of an expedition that explored some of the deepest parts of the Pacific Ocean, near the Galapagos Islands. Using *Alvin*, the team found what looked like clouds of black smoke streaming out of the ocean floor. The smoke was actually hot water that had come from below the ocean's floor and was filled with minerals. As the mineral-rich water cooled, it formed solid shafts. Scientists called the shafts hydrothermal vents and gave them the nickname "black smokers". The scientists were surprised to find that previously unknown sea creatures lived near them. Among them were giant clams and long tube worms of various colours. The scientists discovered that bacteria that ate the minerals provided a source of food for other sea life. The newly found deep-sea life amazed scientists. They hadn't thought complex life forms could exist without photosynthesis, the process by which plants use sunlight to produce their food.

Inside *Alvin*, the crew saw items on the ocean floor. One was the ceramic head from a doll. The rest of the toy had long ago been eaten by tiny creatures of the deep. Ballard also saw passengers' suitcases and china from the ship's dining rooms, as well as sinks and toilet bowls that had broken free of their plumbing. "Whenever something interesting appeared in my viewport," he later wrote, "we'd slow down so I could snap a picture. The sheer scale of this 'museum' was overwhelming." On another dive, Ballard used a mechanical arm to leave behind plaques to honor the people who died when the *Titanic* sank. He hoped future explorers would not disturb the ship's remains, out of respect for the dead.

A commemorative plaque rests on the deck of the *Titanic*.

"For the
first time,
a remotely
operated
vehicle was
crucial to the
success of a
deep undersea
mission."

When the second mission to the *Titanic* was finished, Ballard began to consider what he had learned. Some of the disaster's eyewitnesses clearly had been right – the ship had broken in two, either just before sinking or as it was going down. From what he and his crew could see, the iceberg did not tear one long gash in the ship's hull. Most of the damaged part of the hull, however, was buried in the mud, so he couldn't tell what had happened. Ballard assumed that water had entered the hull in several places. Probably the water had flooded in at places where the ship's steel plates had pulled apart.

Knowing where the *Titanic* sank, Ballard considered the debate over the role of the *Californian* on the night of 14 April 1912. The two ships were further apart than the *Titanic*'s officers had thought. But they were still close enough for the crew on the *Californian* to see the rockets the *Titanic* launched. Ballard concluded that whatever the distance, the crew of the *Californian* "failed to act when action was called for".

Ballard also reflected on what he and his crew had accomplished on their two expeditions. Their success showed the value of using both sound – sonar – and sight – video cameras – to find underwater wrecks. He added, "For the first time, a remotely operated vehicle was crucial to the success of a deep undersea mission."

ChapterFour
THE FASCINATION CONTINUES

Although Robert Ballard tried to keep the location of the *Titanic* to himself, the information was not a secret for long. The first commercial dive to the wreck site took place in 1987. Using the French submersible *Nautile*, employees of a US company retrieved more than 800 artifacts, including a signal bell, a porthole frame, a silver tray and dishes. *Nautile*, like *Alvin*, had a three-man crew and could reach depths of nearly 6 km (4 miles). The crew used their mini-sub's mechanical arm to pick up the items and place them in a basket outside *Nautile*. The crew videotaped its work and the wreckage with a camera designed for American space shuttle missions.

Ballard was not the only person who opposed disturbing the *Titanic*'s final resting place. Edith Haisman was 15 years old in 1912 and a *Titanic* passenger. She sat in a lifeboat in the early hours of 15 April as she watched the ship sink with her father still on board. When the *Nautile* carried out its mission, Haisman was 90, and she said, "Everything should be left exactly where it is." The firm behind the expedition, however, said the project was historically important.

One surprise came when the *Nautile*'s crew found a leather bag. Chemicals used to tan the leather had

The ship's bell that rang moments before the *Titanic* hit an iceberg was retrieved from the sunken ship. It is exhibited around the world with other artifacts.

helped preserve it. The tiny sea creatures that ate parts of much of the ship and its artifacts stayed away from the bag because of the chemicals. Inside it were coins and jewellery covered with diamonds and other gems. Preserving these and other artifacts was a challenge for the team's research scientists. After being in the dark salt water for so long, the artifacts could have crumbled to pieces when exposed to gases in the air. The items were packed in salt water and shipped to a French lab, which had developed special techniques for preserving delicate artifacts. Sending an electric current through the *Titanic*'s artifacts removed the salts in them, which otherwise would have reacted with the hydrogen and oxygen in the air and created a destructive acid.

The *Nautile* mission led its backers to suggest that the iceberg alone had not brought down the *Titanic*. The appearance of part of the hull indicated that there had been an explosion inside the ship. George Tulloch, one of the investors, thought the collision with the ice caused a spark in a coal bin, triggering an explosion. Robert Ballard quickly rejected that theory, and it's not widely accepted today. Some eyewitnesses did report hearing explosions as the ship sank, but not before. Others said the sounds they had heard were more like rumbling or the noise of something being crushed.

A recent documentary film has revived the idea that the collision alone did not sink the ship. An Irish journalist says the disaster was accelerated by a huge coal fire in the hull that had started three weeks before the *Titanic* set sail. "It's a perfect storm of extraordinary factors coming together: fire, ice and criminal negligence," said Senan Molony of the *Irish Daily Mail* in the documentary

The *Titanic* was built at the Harland and Wolff shipyards in Belfast, Northern Ireland.

Titanic: The New Evidence. "The fire was known about, but it was played down. She should never have been put to sea." Recently discovered photographs of the *Titanic* before it set sail reveal a long black mark on the ship's hull, near the area that was hit by the iceberg. Experts believe the mark was mostly likely made by a fire in the ship.

Several more expeditions followed the *Nautile* mission in the 1990s. One used two new Russian submersibles, *Mir I* and *Mir II*, to explore the wreck and film it for IMAX movie theatres. Ralph White, a *National Geographic* photographer who had been one of the filmmakers on the *Knorr* in 1985, took part in the filming of the IMAX film, called *Titanica*. He had also taken part in the 1987 salvaging expedition. Along with Emory Kristof, White helped create most of the new technology used for underwater camera work on the missions to explore the *Titanic*.

Ralph White photographed the *Titanic*'s front mast smashed upon the sunken ship's upper deck.

For *Titanica*, White and his crew used one mini-sub to light the wreck with powerful lights, while a camera in the other filmed it. White later said, "I couldn't believe how clear the images were." Film critic Roger Ebert wrote that "the result is positively eerie: At a depth where no sunlight at all penetrates, the subs, sometimes working together, are able to light up the area so effectively that we see clearly as we drift above the bones of the great ship." One finding from the mission was that the *Titanic* fortunately landed in an excellent spot for it to be discovered. Most of the ocean floor near it was so soft, one scientist said, that it might have sunk out of sight if it had landed elsewhere.

On his various missions, White also took still pictures, which appeared in newspapers and books. He made more than 30 dives to the wreck in submersibles during his career. With the many hours he had spent on the wreck, he sometimes joked that he had spent more time on the *Titanic* than Captain Edward Smith did.

The company that carried out the 1987 mission returned to the site several times in the 1990s. A US court said the business, now called RMS Titanic Inc., was the only company allowed to salvage artifacts from the area of the wreckage. The later dives brought thousands more artifacts to the surface. RMS Titanic could show the artifacts in public, but it was not allowed to sell them. The money it made from exhibits of the artifacts helped pay for future dives.

Perhaps the most famous dive of that decade was used to film parts of what became one of the most popular films of all time. In 1991 filmmaker James Cameron was trying to decide what to do for his next project. His popular film *Terminator 2: Judgment Day* had just been released. Cameron had long been interested in underwater exploration. As a teenager he had learned to scuba dive, and he made a model of a device called Sublimnos, which he built to test how

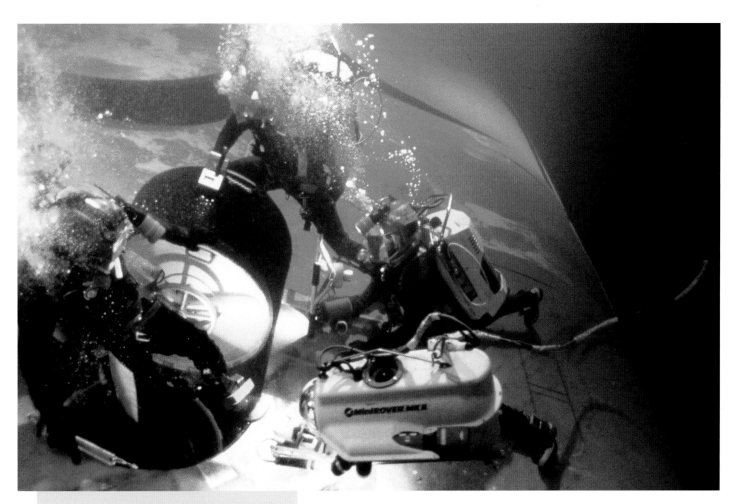

A remotely operated vehicle in James Cameron's _The Abyss_ was nicknamed _Little Geek._

well people could live underwater. While still at high school, Cameron wrote a short story about a researcher working in a structure something like Sublimnos. The story later inspired his film _The Abyss_, which was shot mainly in a large tank filled with water. The film showed two remotely operated vehicles that were based somewhat on the ROVs Ballard had used to find and explore the _Titanic_.

Cameron knew something about the sinking of the great ship, but he decided to make a film about it after watching _A Night to Remember_ for the first time in

20 years. He thought that combining the events of April 1912 with the explorations of the *Titanic* wreck would make a great story. When he saw the IMAX movie *Titanica*, he realized he could use the two *Mir* submersibles to make the film.

Cameron set off on his first mission to film the *Titanic* in 1995. Because of his previous success as a filmmaker, he had plenty of money to spend, and he needed it. He designed and built a new film camera that would work in the extreme depths of the ocean. When the Woods Hole Oceanographic Institution wouldn't let him use *Jason Jr*, he had his own remotely operated vehicle built. His ROV "didn't have to be the best exploration vehicle in history," Cameron later wrote, "it just needed to work long enough to appear in a few key shots." Shooting his underwater scenes, Cameron went deeper into the ship than Ballard's teams had. His ROV, called *Snoop Dog*, discovered a fireplace in one of the first-class cabins. Leaving that space, however, the ROV's cable got caught around a post, and it took its pilot about an hour to free the vehicle. Despite that problem, Cameron decided he would return to the *Titanic* to explore more of what was inside the wreck.

Cameron's *Titanic* was released in 1997. It was a hit around the world, earning more than $2 billion (£1.5 billion). It also won 11 Academy Awards, including Best Picture. In his film, Cameron included

Shooting his underwater scenes, Cameron went deeper into the ship than Ballard's teams had.

FROM THE DIRECTOR OF 'ALIENS,' 'T2' AND 'TRUE LIES'

LEONARDO DiCAPRIO · KATE WINSLET

TITANIC

NOTHING ON EARTH COULD COME BETWEEN THEM.

Titanic was the highest-grossing film of all time until Cameron's *Avatar* surpassed it in 2010.

a fictional love story about a wealthy passenger, played by Kate Winslet, and a poor third-class passenger, played by Leonardo DiCaprio. Along with telling their story and showing in great detail the sinking of the *Titanic*, the movie featured some of the footage Cameron had shot of the wreck.

By the time *Titanic* came out, another expedition had gone down to the wreck site. This time, RMS

Titanic wanted more than just artifacts. It planned to retrieve a large steel piece from the ship's hull, which its crews had first seen in 1994. On a 1996 expedition, the company attached flotation balloons filled with diesel fuel – which is lighter than water – to the steel piece to float it to the surface. Passengers aboard two cruise ships overhead watched the retrieval effort on TV screens.

RMS Titanic managed to raise the piece of steel to about 64 m (210 feet) below the ocean's surface. But the seas became choppy, and several cables attaching the balloons to the piece broke. The steel plunged 4 km (2.5 miles) back to the ocean bottom. The failed effort lessened some of Ballard's interest in exploring the site again. He wrote later that the salvagers "profess respect for the site's historical importance but more often demonstrate careless disregard."

RMS Titanic tried again to snag the section of the ship's hull in 1998. This time it successfully retrieved what is known as the "Big Piece", a 13.6-metric tonne (15-ton) hunk of steel. It includes all or part of six portholes, with the glass still in place in three of them. After the Big Piece was treated so it wouldn't fall apart, it went on display in Las Vegas, Nevada, USA, with other *Titanic* artifacts. Later it was shown at other sites.

After the success of *Titanic*, James Cameron decided he wanted to film the wreck site again.

A FREQUENT VISITOR

Divers successfully raised part of the Titanic's *hull known as the "Big Piece".*

Robert Ballard and James Cameron are the most famous explorers of the *Titanic* wreck. But the person said to have made the most trips to the site is Paul-Henry Nargeolet. A veteran of the French navy, he once searched for explosives in the water before learning how to pilot submersibles. In 1987 Nargeolet led the first salvaging mission for the company that later became RMS Titanic Inc. He went to the site four more times, making several dives each time. Nargeolet led the expedition that found the "Big Piece" of the ship's hull. He was also on the 2010 expedition that made the detailed map of the site,

and he once searched the ocean for a missing jet airliner. Nargeolet knows that Ballard and others have criticized his salvaging work. But he said some survivors have thanked him for his efforts. "My belief is that it is good to record the artifacts, that it's good for education and preservation," Nargeolet said in 2012. "That's the goal."

The *Titanic*'s last survivor, Millvina Dean, died in 2009 at age 97. She was only 2 months old when the ship went down, the youngest passenger aboard. Dean's mother and brother also survived, but her father died when the ship sank.

This time he would use 3D footage for a documentary film that would be called *Ghosts of the Abyss*. After his ROV *Snoop Dog* got tangled during the 1995 expedition, Cameron had a new ROV built. Instead of drawing electric power from a cable attached to a submersible, the new model would carry batteries. That would let Cameron use a very thin, long tether that only had to transmit information through a glass wire called a fibre-optic cable. Fibre optics can be used to send information long distances. The information, in digital form, is transmitted by light. Cameron's new ROVs would carry a tether thousands of metres long, which the robot itself would unwind as it moved. As Cameron later explained, "Then the vehicle can go into the wreck, wrap 10 times around a post, go down a stairwell, go down a hallway, explore for hours, and then find a completely different path to come back out of the ship." Once back at the submersible, the crew would simply cut the tether, because fibre optic cable is cheap and a new one can be used for the next dive. With that process, the ROV's pilot did not have to retrace the ROV's path to free it from any tangles.

Working with his brother Mike, an engineer, Cameron created several of the new-generation ROVs, which they called Spider-bots. They set the lights and cameras farther apart than on older ROVs, which allowed for clearer filming underwater. In 2001, using

The *Mir I* and *Mir II* submersibles carried Cameron's team on 12 dives to the *Titanic* wreck during the filming of *Ghosts of the Abyss.*

the Spider-bots, Cameron explored further into the wreck than he had before.

Cameron went back to film the wreck one more time, in 2005. On that mission, as on the one in 2001, scientist Lori Johnston went along to study the bacteria on the wreck and to learn how they were destroying it. Some of the bacteria formed the rusticles that Robert Ballard had discovered. Others formed what Johnston called "slime clouds" that floated in the water and fed on wood and metal in the ship. Some clouds were clear, some were foggy, some even had a bit of colour, and all were very mobile.

But Johnston saw very few other aquatic creatures at the *Titanic* site, apart from rattail fish, small starfish and crabs.

After staying away from the *Titanic* for almost 20 years, Robert Ballard finally returned to the wreck in 2004. He went as part of a mission sponsored by the National Oceanographic and Atmospheric Administration, which carried out two expeditions to the *Titanic* in the early 2000s. On the 2004 trip, NOAA scientists wanted to study the tiny sea life that was eating away the ship. Ballard wanted to examine the wreck with high-definition video technology, which was new at the time. He later wrote, "We were going to bring up the cleanest, clearest images yet of the ship."

RMS Titanic and the Woods Hole Oceanographic Institute sent an expedition down in 2010 to map the area around the *Titanic* in the greatest detail ever. Using sonar and ROVs that took more than 130,000 pictures, the scientists mapped an area of 39 square km (15 square miles). For the first time, autonomous underwater vehicles visited the site. These vehicles have computers that let them move on their own, without being controlled by humans nearby. Seeing more details of the wreckage gave scientists new understanding about the ship's sinking. David Alberg of NOAA said, "You really begin to understand how violently the ship tore itself apart when it went down

Robert Ballard gestured to a large-scale photo of the *Titanic*'s upper deck during an appearance in 2012, the 100th anniversary of the ship's sinking.

and landed all over this enormous footprint on the bottom of the ocean."

The results of the 2010 mapping were released in 2012, the 100th anniversary of the sinking of the *Titanic*. That year, the United Nations Educational, Scientific and Cultural Organization (UNESCO) said the wreck site was protected under a 2001 international agreement meant to preserve underwater sites of historical importance. Many nations had not signed the agreement, however, and there was no guarantee that salvagers would stop going to the ship.

Preserving the wreck site has become a major concern for Ballard and other scientists. On his 2004 trip, Ballard could see the damage human activity was doing to the site. ROVs and submersibles sometimes banged into the ship. Ballard wrote that some expeditions to the site had been careful, while others had not, meaning that "the long-term effect of all these visits to the wreck has been to speed up the ship's natural decay."

On the 2010 expedition, scientists discovered a new type of bacteria living on the rusticles that surround parts of the wrecked ship. The bacteria eat both the iron in many parts of the ship and the rust that forms on it. One scientist who studied the bacteria predicted that within 20 years, all that might be left of the ship is a rust stain on the ocean floor. To help slow the natural decay of the *Titanic*, Ballard has suggested coating parts of the wreck with a paint that keeps the bacteria from eating away at the ship.

Throughout his career, Robert Ballard made important contributions to underwater technology and scientific exploration. But he will always be best known for discovering the *Titanic*. Thanks to his first two expeditions, people finally knew what happened to the ship after survivors saw it plunge into the icy Atlantic. The discovery also showed the role that ROVs could play in ocean research. People in 1912 put too much faith in modern engineering when they

The slant of rusticles indicated the direction of the current as a submersible illuminated the *Titanic*'s bow.

called the *Titanic* unsinkable. Human error and nature can work together to create disasters, as they did more than 100 years ago. But modern technology has worked well in opening the previously unseen world beneath the sea.

Ballard searched for the *Titanic*, in part, to prove the value of that technology. His success also renewed interest in the many stories that have swirled about the *Titanic*, its passengers, and its crew. People all over the world can see the artifacts salvaged from the wreck and relive the mystery and horror of the iceberg crash. Those pieces of the past help keep alive the memory of the ship and the victims of the disaster.

Timeline

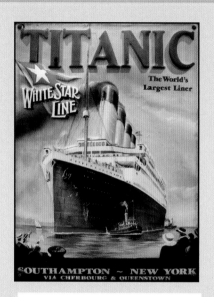

10 April 1912

The *Titanic* sails on its first voyage

14 April 1912

The ship hits an iceberg and sinks early in the morning of 15 April; of the more than 2,200 passengers and crew, only 705 survive

1980

Jack Grimm makes the first of three unsuccessful attempts to find the *Titanic*

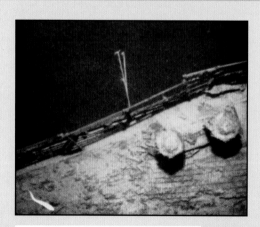

1985

On 1 September, Ballard and his crew find the *Titanic* using the submersible *Argo*

1958

The film *A Night to Remember*, based on a 1955 book, stirs new interest in the *Titanic*

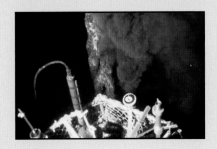

1977

Robert Ballard makes his first attempt to find the wreck of the *Titanic*; Ballard and other scientists discover black smokers deep underwater

1986

Using the submersible *Alvin* and the ROV *Jason Jr*, Ballard further explores the wreck

1987

The first salvaging mission goes to the *Titanic* and returns with more than 800 artifacts

Timeline

1995

The IMAX film *Titanica* shows detailed images of the wreck; James Cameron films the wreck for a film he is making

1996

The salvaging company RMS Titanic Inc. fails to bring a 13.6-metric tonne (15-ton) piece of *Titanic*'s hull to the surface but succeeds two years later

2004

Working with the US government, Ballard returns to the *Titanic* for the first time since 1986

2005

Cameron again films the wreck of the *Titanic*

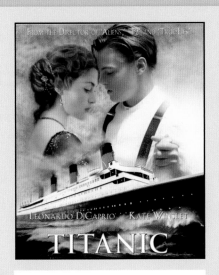

2001

Cameron returns to the wreck to shoot footage for his 3D film *Ghosts of the Abyss*

1997

Cameron's movie *Titanic* is released and becomes a hit

2017

A documentary reveals that newly discovered photos possibly indicate that a fire in the *Titanic*'s hull contributed to the ship's sinking

2010

RMS Titanic Inc. and the Woods Hole Oceanographic Institution work together to create the most detailed map of the wreck site ever made

Glossary

artifact object made by a person, typically an item of cultural or historical interest

autonomous able to act independently; automous robots are not operated remotely by people

bacteria tiny life forms

crow's nest lookout post high above the rest of a ship

debris remains of something broken or destroyed

expedition trip taken by a group of people for a specific purpose, such as exploration or scientific research

hull main body of a ship or boat below the main deck, including its bottom and sides

nuclear having to do with the energy created by splitting atoms; submarines can use the energy created by nuclear reactors as a power source

oceanographer scientist who studies oceanic plant and animal life, rock formations and other parts of the ocean

salvage rescue a wrecked or disabled ship or its cargo from loss at sea

sonar device that uses sound waves to find underwater objects; sonar stands for sound navigation and ranging

submersible small vessels used under water, usually for research

tether rope, cable or chain used to keep things tied together

Additional resources

Further Reading

MacKay, J. (2014) *James Cameron.*
Detroit: Lucent Books.

Mara, W. (2015) *Deep-Sea Exploration: Science, Technology and Engineering.*
New York: Children's Press.

Otfinoski, S. (2016) *Smooth Sea and a Fighting Chance: The Story of the Sinking of* Titanic.
Oxford: Raintree Publishers.

Spilsbury, R. and Spilsbury, L. (2016) *Robots Underwater.* New York: Gareth Stevens Publishing.

Websites

www.bbc.co.uk/history/titanic
Learn more about the *Titanic*, including its construction in Belfast and the dives made to the wreckage. Watch an animation of the lifespan of the ship.

http://www.rmg.co.uk/discover/explore/sea-ships/titanic
Discover how key objects help reveal the *Titanic*'s story, and find out more about life at the time *Titanic* set sail.

Critical thinking questions

The sinking of the *Titanic* on its maiden voyage shocked the world. Why were people stunned when they learned of the disaster?

Many lives were lost when the *Titanic* went down. Could more lives have been saved? How? Is someone in particular at fault for the huge loss of life?

Do you agree with Robert Ballard that people should not have removed items from the wreckage of the *Titanic* or disturbed it in any way? Why or why not?

Source notes

Page 6, line 26: Robert Ballard and Rick Archbold. *Robert Ballard's Titanic*. New York: Barnes & Noble, 2007, p. 54.

Page 10, line 12: Ibid., p. 77.

Page 11, col. 2, line 4: John Roach. "Titanic Was Found During Secret Cold War Navy Mission." *National Geographic*. 2 June 2008. 15 Nov. 2016. http://news.nationalgeographic.com/news/2008/06/080602-titanic-secret.html

Page 12, line 5: Ibid., p. 80.

Page 12, line 21: Ibid., p. 82.

Page 13, line 5: Ibid., p. 83.

Page 16, line 12: Walter Lord. *The Night Lives On*. New York: Morrow, 1986, p. 28.

Page 16, line 20: Richard Davenport-Hines. *Voyagers of the Titanic: Passengers, Sailors, Shipbuilders, Aristocrats, and the Worlds They Came From*. New York: William Morrow, 2012, p. 109.

Page 17, line 6: *The Night Lives On*, p. 69.

Page 22, line 2: *Voyagers of the Titanic: Passengers, Sailors, Shipbuilders, Aristocrats, and the Worlds They Came From*, p. 232.

Page 22, line 13: "The Appalling Disaster." *The New York Times*. 16 April 1912, p. 12.

Page 22, line 17: Ibid.

Page 23, line 3: "British Wreck Commissioner's Inquiry: Report on the Loss of the 'Titanic.'" 30 July 1912. Titanic Inquiry Project. 15 Nov. 2016. http://www.titanicinquiry.org/BOTInq/BOTReport/botRep01.php

Page 26, col. 1, line 9: Steven Crandell. "Exploring the Deep Ocean—Emory Kristof's Pioneering Photography." *The Huffington Post*. 21 April 2011. 15 Nov. 2016. http://www.huffingtonpost.com/steven-crandell/emory-kristof_b_849437.html

Page 26, col. 2, line 6: *Robert Ballard's Titanic*, p. 36.

Page 28, line 12: Ibid., p. 84.

Page 34, line 8: William Sellers. "A Titanic Tale: A former *Alvin* pilot recalls his 1986 dives on the shipwreck." *Oceanus Magazine*. 2 Sept. 2010. 15 Nov. 2016. http://www.whoi.edu/oceanus/feature/a-titanic-tale

Page 34, caption, line 2: James B. Meigs. "Exploring with Video." *Popular Mechanics*. November 1986, p. 22.

Page 36, line 7: *Robert Ballard's Titanic*, p. 149.

Page 37, line 20: Ibid., p. 200.

Page 37, line 26: Ibid., p. 211.

Page 38, line 20: Sydney Rubin. "Treasures of the Titanic: Priceless artifacts return from the lost liner's deep-sea grave." *Popular Mechanics*. December 1987, p. 66.

Page 40, line 25: Dan Bilefsky. "Coal Fire, Not Just Iceberg, Doomed the Titanic, a Journalist Claims." *The New York Times*. 3 Jan. 2017. 18 Jan. 2017. https://www.nytimes.com/2017/01/03/world/europe/titanic-coal-fire-iceberg.html?emc=edit_nn_20170104&nl=morning-briefing&nlid=56738233&te=1

Page 43, line 4: Jocelyn Y. Stewart. "Ralph Bradshaw White, 1941-2008: Explorer Filmed the Wreckage of Titanic." *Los Angeles Times*. 13 Feb. 2008. 15 Nov. 2016. http://articles.latimes.com/2008/feb/13/local/me-white13

Page 43, line 5: Roger Ebert. "Titanica." Roger Ebert.com. 14 April 1995. 15 Nov. 2016. http://www.rogerebert.com/reviews/titanica-1995.

Page 46, line 13: *James Cameron. Exploring the Deep: The Titanic Expeditions*. San Rafael, Calif.: Insight Editions, 2013, p. 42.

Page 48, line 15: *Robert Ballard's Titanic*, p. 213.

Page 49, col. 2, line 4: Monte Burke. "Meet the Titanic's Greatest Explorer (No, It Isn't James Cameron)." *Forbes*. 30 March 2012. 15 Nov. 2016. http://www.forbes.com/sites/monteburke/2012/03/30/meet-the-titanics-greatest-explorer/#72bdd3867619

Page 50, line 14: *Exploring the Deep: The Titanic Expeditions*, p. 58.

Page 51, line 9: Ibid., p. 152.

Page 52, line 13: Robert Ballard and Ian Coutts. *Titanic: The Last Great Images*. Philadelphia: Running Press, 2008, p. 10.

Page 52, line 27: Jennie Cohen. "First Map of Entire Titanic Wreck Site Sheds New Light on Disaster." History. 8 March 2012. 15 Nov. 2016. http://www.history.com/news/first-map-of-entire-titanic-wreck-site-sheds-new-light-on-disaster

Page 54, line 7: *Titanic: The Last Great Images*, p. 121.

Select bibliography

"The Appalling Disaster." *The New York Times*. 16 April 1912, p. 12.

Ballard, Robert, and Ian Coutts. *Titanic: The Last Great Images*. Philadelphia: Running Press, 2008.

Ballard, Robert, and Rick Archbold. *Robert Ballard's Titanic*. New York: Barnes & Noble, 2007.

Bilefsky, Dan. "Coal Fire, Not Just Iceberg, Doomed the Titanic, a Journalist Claims." *The New York Times*. 3 Jan. 2017. 18 Jan. 2017. https://www.nytimes.com/2017/01/03/world/europe/titanic-coal-fire-iceberg.html?emc=edit_nn_20170104&nl=morning-briefing&nlid=56738233&te=1

"British Wreck Commissioner's Inquiry: Report on the Loss of the 'Titanic.'" 30 July 1912. Titanic Inquiry Project. 15 Nov. 2016. http://www.titanicinquiry.org/BOTInq/BOTReport/botRep01.php

Broad, William J. "Titanic Wreck Was Surprise Yield of Underwater Test for Military." *The New York Times*. 8 Sept. 1985. 15 Nov. 2016. http://www.nytimes.com/1985/09/08/us/titanic-wreck-was-surrise-yield-of-underwater-tests-for-military.html

Burke, Monte. "Meet the Titanic's Greatest Explorer (No, It Isn't James Cameron)." *Forbes*. 30 March 2012. 15 Nov. 2016. http://www.forbes.com/sites/monteburke/2012/03/30/meet-the-titanics-greatest-explorer/#72bdd3867619

Cameron, James. *Exploring the Deep: The Titanic Expeditions*. San Rafael, Calif.: Insight Editions, 2013.

Ciotti, Paul. "Ralph White's Titanic Adventure: A Visit With a Member of the Woods Hole Expedition." *Los Angeles Times*. 27 Oct. 1985. 15 Nov. 2016. http://articles.latimes.com/1985-10-27/magazine/tm-12994_1_woods-hole-group

Cohen, Jennie. "First Map of Entire Titanic Wreck Site Sheds New Light on Disaster." History. 8 March 2012. 15 Nov. 2016. http://www.history.com/news/first-map-of-entire-titanic-wreck-site-sheds-new-light-on-disaster

Crandell, Steven. "Exploring the Deep Ocean—Emory Kristof's Pioneering Photography." *The Huffington Post*. 21 April 2011. 15 Nov. 2016. http://www.huffingtonpost.com/steven-crandell/emory-kristof_b_849437.html

Davenport-Hines, Richard. *Voyagers of the Titanic: Passengers, Sailors, Shipbuilders, Aristocrats, and the Worlds They Came From*. New York: William Morrow, 2012.

Delgado, James P. "Diving on the Titanic." *Archaeology*. Volume 54 Number 1 (January/February 2001). 15 Nov. 2016. http://archive.archaeology.org/0101/etc/titanic1.html

Encyclopedia Titanica. 15 Nov. 2016. https://www.encyclopedia-titanica.org/

Ebert, Roger. "Titanica." Roger Ebert.com. 14 April 1995. 15 Nov. 2016. http://www.rogerebert.com/reviews/titanica-1995

Hamlin, Jesse. "A 15-ton Piece of the Titanic's Hull Finishes Long Journey—from the Bottom of the Ocean to the Top of Metreon." *San Francisco Chronicle*. 20 May 2006. 15 Nov. 2016. http://www.sfgate.com/entertainment/article/A-15-ton-piece-of-the-Titanic-s-hull-finishes-2496984.php

"How Does Pressure Change with Ocean Depth?" National Ocean Service. National Oceanic and Atmosphere Association. 15 Nov. 2016. http://oceanservice.noaa.gov/facts/pressure.html

Lee, Jane J. "New Plans Could Protect the Titanic, 30 Years After It Was Found." *National Geographic*. 1 Sept. 2015. 15 Nov. 2016. http://news.nationalgeographic.com/2015/08/150901-titanic-shipwreck-discovery-30-anniversary-archaeology-oceans-science/

Lord, Walter. *The Night Lives On*. New York: Morrow, 1986.

"Titanic Sinks Four Hours after Hitting Iceberg." *The New York Times*. 16 April 1912, p. 1.

"Platforms: Submersibles." National Oceanic and Atmospheric Administration. 15 Nov. 2016. http://oceanexplorer.noaa.gov/technology/subs/subs.html

RMS Titanic. 15 Nov. 2016. Woods Hole Oceanographic Institution. https://www.whoi.edu/main/topic/titanic

Roach, John. "Titanic Was Found During Secret Cold War Navy Mission." *National Geographic*. 2 June 2008. 15 Nov. 2016. http://news.nationalgeographic.com/news/2008/06/080602-titanic-secret.html

Rubin, Sydney. "Treasures of the Titanic: Priceless artifacts return from the lost liner's deep-sea grave." *Popular Mechanics*. December 1987, pp. 64-69.

Sellers, William. "A Titanic Tale: A former Alvin pilot recalls his 1986 dives on the shipwreck." *Oceanus Magazine*. 2 Sept. 2010. 15 Nov. 2016. http://www.whoi.edu/oceanus/feature/a-titanic-tale

"Side Scan Sonar." Office of Coast Survey. NOAA. 15 Nov. 2016. http://www.nauticalcharts.noaa.gov/hsd/SSS.html

Smith, Graham. "First it was an iceberg, now it's bacteria: Rust-eating species 'will destroy wreck of Titanic within 20 years.'" *Daily Mail*. 12 Jan. 2011. 15 Nov. 2016. http://www.dailymail.co.uk/sciencetech/article-1346446/Titanic-wreck-completely-destroyed-20-years-new-rust-eating-bacteria.html#ixzz4NNEsRDds

Stewart, Jocelyn Y. "Ralph Bradshaw White, 1941–2008: Explorer Filmed the Wreckage of Titanic." *Los Angeles Times*. 13 Feb. 2008. 15 Nov. 2016. http://articles.latimes.com/2008/feb/13/local/me-white13

Sullivan, Walter. "Blast Theory in Titanic's Sinking Is Disputed." *The New York Times*. 1 Nov. 1987. 15 Nov. 2016. http://www.nytimes.com/1987/11/01/us/blast-theory-in-titanic-s-sinking-is-disputed.html

Titanic: The Artifact Exhibition. Premier Exhibitions. 24 March 2017. http://www.premierexhibitions.com/exhibitions/3/3/titanic-artifact-exhibition

Titanic Universe. 24 March 2017. http://www.titanicuniverse.com/

"What is sonar?" National Ocean Service. NOAA. 15 Nov. 2016. http://oceanservice.noaa.gov/facts/sonar.html

Index

About the author

Michael Burgan has written many books for children and young adults during his 20 years as a freelance writer. Most of his books have focused on history. Burgan has won several awards for his writing. He lives in Santa Fe, New Mexico, USA.